A GUIDE TO WILDERNESS CANOE FISHING

by
Frank R. Richards

Copyright © 2011 Frank R Richards
All rights reserved.
ISBN: 1467902926
ISBN 13: 9781467902922
Library of Congress Control Number: 2011960376
CreateSpace, North Charleston, SC

DEDICATION

This book is dedicated to my childhood friends and original fishing buddies: Steve, Andy, Norman, and Ralph. We grew up together in the rural community of Andover, New Hampshire, where we attended a two-room schoolhouse through the sixth grade.

I don't think any of us realized where the magic of those early experiences would lead. We were just kids, going fishing within walking distance of our homes.

Norman became an expert fly fisherman who founded an international guiding service, Streamside Adventures, as a retirement project. Steve eventually became the president of the Andover Fish and Game Club. Ralph enjoyed a career in forestry.

I discovered wilderness canoeing in the mid-1970s. Andy quickly became my regular partner. We've been friends since we were two, and we've been going on canoe trips since our twenties. We've reached our sixties now, and we're not done yet.

ACKNOWLEDGMENTS

I'd like to thank the aforementioned Norman, Norman Crisp, for providing information about the layer of calm water underneath a rapid.

I'd like to thank Charles "Bassenstose" Backenstose for information about spinnerbaits.

I'd like to thank Jeff Levesque for showing me how effective plugs can be in heavy current.

I'd like to thank the many canoeing guides I've booked with over the years, particularly Bob Barnes, Randy Cross, Eric LeClair, Nels Liljedah, David Morin, and Dwayne Shaw. They made it possible for me to take things to a whole different level.

INTRODUCTION

I will always be grateful to the friends who invited me to go on my first canoe trip—a classic beer float on the Upper Iowa River. Something about the experience appealed to me immediately. I still remember sitting beside a flickering fire on a sandbar, looking over dark water into the night, and thinking, "I'm going to be doing more of this."

Another invitation soon led me to the Boundary Waters Wilderness Canoe Area between Minnesota and Ontario. That excursion was the first gateway on a journey that will continue until the aging process brings me to my bed. After that trip, canoe travel in the north woods became almost an addiction for me.

I had good memories of fishing when I was a kid. For no greater reason, I began taking a rod and reel along on my canoe trips. I quickly reconnected with the interest I had felt during my childhood.

Fishing proved to be another gateway to the fascination of the wilderness. As an adult, the whole experience was incredibly stimulating. The search process, using logic to find fish, was like solving an intriguing puzzle. The strike, the fight, the landing, and even the release were exciting in a primitive, visceral way.

That reaction is commonplace. I think it reflects our evolutionary history as hunter-gatherers. It is an emotional reaction to capturing prey, possibly imprinted into our DNA.

Remote water is a sacred place to reconnect with our ancestral identity, including our experience of being the apex predator. Fishing is, however, a secondary activity on a canoe trip. You need to plan carefully to make time for it. You need to develop skills and acquire proper equipment.

I had the good fortune to meet a guide on one of my early visits to the Boundary Waters. Our groups had come together on a portage, and we made a little small talk at the end.

This guide's personality was friendly, even slightly extroverted. His appearance suggested that he was highly experienced. His leather vest and turquoise studded belt bespoke a connection to the native peoples, and I thought he was almost surely from the nearby Chippewa settlement. I don't think his clients understood they were out with a pro, someone who could make everything look easy. His clients seemed surprised when I told them I'd only caught a few fish.

I was a rank beginner, using cheap spinning gear, the kind you buy in a convenience store for about twenty dollars. I joked about not knowing how to fish. The guide laughed with me and said, "It takes a while."

I eventually came to believe that his comment, in addition to being nice, was a sophisticated observation by a person who knew. Thirty years later, I am still learning different, interesting things regularly.

That conversation with the guide occurred in 1982. I have taken a canoeing vacation almost every year since, and I have seen beautiful places and have enjoyed good fishing.

I slowly learned the basics of sport angling and developed a system adapted to canoes and wilderness tripping. This book is meant to share that set of ideas and, perhaps, speed up the learning process for someone who is just getting started. I hope the material helps my readers enjoy this mesmerizing activity. By the time they finish the book, I hope they feel as though they got their money's worth.

Good fishing, and enjoy the journey.

CHAPTER 1

FISHING AND CANOE TRIPPING

Experiencing a fishery not subject to heavy angling pressure is one of the luxuries of canoe travel in the deep woods. Even close to civilization, most likely, you will be the only person casting to a spot on a given day. Farther into the bush, you may be the only one to try your luck in a week, a month, or even longer.

Although more and bigger fish are likely to be available, a canoeist-angler must work on many practical issues before starting out.

For example, a fitness-oriented lifestyle is almost mandatory. Canoe travel and camping are demanding. If you are out of shape, you will be too tired to enjoy the day, much less enjoy fishing.

Obviously, it is a good idea to know how to paddle, but expect it to be more difficult than it may look at first. Taking lessons can be extremely helpful. Similarly, efficient camping practices are important. The less time and energy spent on the basics of cooking, cleaning dishes, gathering firewood—the more you will be able to focus on angling.

Less obvious is the need to learn how to estimate time and distance. If your trip plan proves ill-conceived, you will need to paddle hard from dawn to dusk in order to complete your route. Such a miscalculation can take the joy right out of the experience.

Scheduling time to fish can be surprisingly challenging. For example, only a few people in a group may be interested. If your companions want to paddle hard all day and cover a good distance, you may be limited to a few impromptu casts. Even with motivated partners, recreational angling and canoe travel do not mix well. It's almost impossible to fish and also cover many miles on a given day.

So, the first trip to an area is always exploratory in nature. Enjoy those occasional casts. Be at peace with the idea that you won't be able to fish anywhere nearly as much as you would like.

Think about the next time you'll be able to visit the same area. Once you have a good idea where the best sections are, it is easier to plan a second trip with the goal of fishing.

Scheduling about one-third the normal distance to be covered in a day usually provides adequate opportunities for fishing. You may not be able to shorten a route by that much, but any extra time can always be put to good use.

Generally, I think focusing on the water near your campsite is the best way to combine fishing and canoe touring. Try to stop early in a good place, make camp, eat, and relax. Then, fish in the evening and in the morning.

There's nothing wrong with getting started at eleven o'clock instead of at nine. Similarly, there's nothing wrong with stopping to camp at three o'clock instead of at five.

Wilderness fishing is different than fishing at home with motorized boats and electronic fish finders. Adapting to an unpredictable schedule and a canoe filled with camping gear does take a while. It is, however, a great way to spend time.

CHAPTER 2

CANOE ADAPTATION

Canoes are designed for efficient paddling rather than sport angling, but when conditions are calm enough for the stern paddler to control, a canoe can be an effective fishing platform.

On lakes, paddling along the shoreline is usually the best way to find good fishing spots, but many good places exist farther out. Without a motor and electronics, however, they may prove difficult to locate.

On rivers, the current provides important clues and is usually a key factor in assessing whether an area may hold fish. Generally, it is easier to locate good places on rivers because the current provides so much information. For example, you can see water moving on the inside and outside of eddies and you can deduce where there may be fish holding areas underneath rapids.

I think a bass boat provides a good template for assessing potential fishing spots on either rivers or lakes. Elevated above, a tournament style pro boat can use an electric motor to adjust position and cast from a perfect distance. An angler can quickly test all the potential spots in a section of water this way.

In a tandem canoe, anglers can mimic this approach by using the rear paddler as the human equivalent of an electric motor. When on the fishing grounds, the person in back should concentrate on positioning the boat and maintaining stability. The person in front should cast to logical targets, emphasizing water near the shoreline.

The rear angler can fish a little by using a rod holder to suspend a lure about a foot below the surface. This rig almost never snags or needs attention. "Dangling" isn't as productive as casting, but it can surprise you. Fish see the silhouette of the lure above them and rise quickly from the depths below. They will come up, seemingly out of nowhere, and just nail this passive lure.

If the front angler hooks a fish, the rear angler should remove their outfit from the rod holder, cast, retrieve, and try to keep the lure close to the hooked fish. Fish are aggressive and competitive, and often several will congregate in an area. They hone in on the struggle, looking to steal food. So, this second rig stands a good chance of picking up a strike.

There's no harm in both paddlers taking a few casual casts at the same time. If real fishing is on the agenda, however, the above system will produce much better results. Anglers usually switch places at regular intervals. It just takes a minute to cruise to shore and swap seats.

CHAPTER 3

THE IMPORTANCE OF FINDING GOOD PLACES

A fish will usually attack anything that even looks like it might be food. Novice anglers, even small children, can do well if they are in a good spot. I learned this through an embarrassingly bad cast, but I humbly accepted the lesson.

We had been traveling on a small river. Short class II rapids impounded long pools behind them. Willow and dogwood trees lined the banks. Occasionally, a stand of pines appeared on higher ground. We stopped early at one of these places, pitched our tents, took a swim, and ate supper. It was a beautiful evening. While the sun was still up, and the temperature cool and comfortable, I decided to spend a little time casting from shore.

A tree on the other side had fallen in, almost perpendicular to the bank. Most of it rested in four to five feet of water, with an eddy behind the log. Nearby, the water was shallow, maybe two feet deep. Even a novice like me instinctively knew this was a good place.

This spot was unusual because I could see all three features: the log, the eddy, and deeper water adjacent to shallow. Together, they produced a neon sign announcing, "Fish Here."

I cast, aiming near the bank next to the fallen tree. Unfortunately, my rod hit a branch. My float and bait, a night crawler, landed way off to the side. They made a loud splash. I swore.

Then, to my astonishment, a piscine torpedo erupted from underneath the log. I watched its black shadow travel at warp speed and strike hard. A few minutes later, I was releasing a smallmouth bass and smiling.

I had miscast so badly it was disheartening, but at that particular spot such a gross failure of technique just didn't matter.

This experience impressed a basic principle upon me. The biggest problem is finding places with fish. Technique and equipment count, but they are secondary.

CHAPTER 4

VISUALIZATION AND INTERPRETATION

Finding good spots is difficult because no one can see what lies below the surface. Additionally, a canoeist, most likely, has never fished a particular area before. How should one proceed, lacking prior information or experience?

I gained insight into this while snorkel diving in a small bay near my home. To my surprise, I found fish holding in spots no larger than a closet. Each good place was characterized by two or more features coming together.

The most common features to look for are depth changes, edges where different kinds of bottom meet, rocky areas, underwater objects, weed beds, tributaries, submerged creek channels, current lines, eddies, and the calmer layer of water underneath current.

While snorkel diving, I floated around an area about the size of two football fields. Looking through the mask, I had a panoramic view of the underwater landscape below the surface.

Nothing looked productive. The bottom was flat and mostly clay. I had to go out a long distance to reach a depth of six feet.

Come to find out, however, there was a drop-off within that seemingly featureless expanse. It lay near where the shoreline made a right-angle turn as the small bay left the main part of the lake. Water depth quickly went from inches to about four feet.

There were rocks on shore and in the water. The bottom made an abrupt transition to clay near the drop-off. I could see fish. I returned to this same spot with gear on many occasions. More often than not, I would catch a good bass, within two feet of the shore.

This spot actually contained three significant features: the rocks, the change of depth, and the transition from rock to clay. Only rocks, however, were apparent from the surface.

Using logic and imagination, however, an angler could visualize the bottom's possibilities well enough to justify a trial cast. The right-angle turn hinted at something unusual. I could see the contour of the land, which contained a bit of a hill, and could reasonably speculate it might continue as a drop-off. I could also reasonably speculate that an abrupt transition from rock to clay might be hidden beneath the surface. All of this was plenty enough to justify a trial cast.

The second spot held more subtle signs. A small creek entered the bay. The inlet was about ten feet wide and held a partially submerged log, the only other obvious feature. This wasn't a lot to go on, but at least I could see two items of interest.

I couldn't see that spring floods had scoured a channel well over four feet deep. Nearby, however, it was shallow.

I had the log to work with in my thought process. I could see the water was deeper where it was darker. In addition, there was shade. Speculation about spring floods washing out a channel wouldn't have immediately come to mind.

It was, however, a very good place. I have caught many bass and panfish there, close to shore. Although the sheer number of features seems to be the best indicator of whether a spot will be productive, an underwater object, such as a log, is especially auspicious.

The best place in the bay was also related to the old creek bed. After about fifty feet, the channel faded away. Nearby, there was a gradual drop-off. In maybe thirty feet, the depth went from inches to about four feet. Again, rocks and an abrupt edge led to a transition to clay.

Visualization and interpretation both had some limits. I could speculate, however, that there might be a creek channel, and could at least formulate a theory.

The contour of the land was visible on shore and I could plausibly assume the slope might continue into deeper water. Rocks were also visible on shore. I could reasonably guess they would continue and eventually make a transition to clay. Together with the channel, that gave me three possibly significant features coming together.

This is adequate information to lob a lure and test the area. In this instance, it would have uncovered a real hot spot. Schools of bass could often be found at this location.

Applying logical speculation to what you see can help find fish. On unfamiliar water, it is a useful technique to pick high percentage targets for trial casts.

Look with your mind as well as your eyes. Try visualizing yourself floating on the surface with a panoramic swim mask. Imagine what you might see based on cues from the shore.

This is a surprisingly effective way to deduce where two or more features may come together and create a fish holding area. The search starts visually, continues via interpretation, and ends by casting or trolling to test the idea.

CHAPTER 5

CASTING

Casting, in my opinion, is the most efficient way to test a spot and see if it holds fish. Be forewarned, however; your theories are likely to fail, more times than not.

If fish are present, they will usually take a lure immediately. If you don't get a strike on your first cast, it probably means no fish is on that target. Two tries are almost always enough. Moving on quickly improves your odds. The more spots you try the more likely one of them will be productive.

Because you are in a canoe, looking for features close to the shoreline is the best option. On either lakes or rivers, the shore is usually the most available source of information to help you identify possible fish holding locations.

Some types of presentations lend themselves to casting parallel to the shore. Most of the time, however, I think you are better off casting perpendicular, while placing your lure within a foot of land. That is a critical detail.

Fish seem to watch the shoreline. It provides them a backdrop to portray forage. They are ready to rush the silhouette of a minnow, crayfish, or a caterpillar falling out of a tree.

Our piscine friends are where they are for a reason. They are looking for a meal and they tend to feed aggressively. I once caught a nice walleye when I inadvertently cast too far and bounced a jig off a large rock. The fish took it on the rebound just as it splashed back into the water.

What happens if the general area looks promising, but even applying a liberal imagination doesn't yield any clear places to try? In such a case, trolling is a better way to test an area. It is, however, in my opinion, a second, less desirable option.

CHAPTER 6

TROLLING

When there is just no clear place to cast, trolling is a way to cover more territory and increase the odds of encountering a good spot. Trolling is only feasible under calm conditions. Otherwise, it is just too much work to paddle.

As with casting, I think better results occur when the rear person paddles and only dangles a lure. Often, the person sitting in the bow may sit backwards facing the stern. This makes for better conversation as well lure control.

Trolling may not succeed in putting a lure in front of fish, but it is a useful search technique when no logical place to cast exists and you have reason to believe fish are present.

Plugs and floating minnows rarely snag. They are effective in water less than ten feet deep. If the water is deeper, running plugs behind bottom-bouncing sinkers works better.

Although a fish can be anywhere in the water column, they tend to be close to the bottom in deeper water. If it's deeper than ten feet, a bottom-bouncing sinker with a floating minnow running about three feet behind creates an effective search system.

The act of paddling lends itself to slow, erratic trolling. This causes a plug to mimic the natural action of a minnow. A small fish often swims along in spurts, going a few feet then pausing.

At least one landscape feature is needed to develop a trolling strategy. Otherwise, you have no basis for a plan. You aren't really trolling. You are just haphazardly dragging a lure through the water.

I remember a narrow section between two lakes. It was about a hundred yards across and half a mile long. I speculated that fish would naturally migrate from one lake to the other, and if so, they would have to go through this area. One prominent feature, a rocky drop-off paralleled one shoreline.

Nature had probably put something somewhere on that long expanse: an object, an edge where the bottom made a transition from one material to another, or maybe both. I had no way of reliably guessing, however, where fish holding spots might be.

The area in question was near our campsite. Twenty minutes after breakfast, we were on the water and fishing. I used a bottom-bouncing sinker and a floating minnow and sat in the front of the canoe. My paddling partner moved the boat slowly, meandering back and forth over the drop-off.

Within an hour, we made two passes. It was very relaxing and, miracle of god, I picked up three walleyes. They made a delicious early lunch.

I must acknowledge that occasionally random trolling can work. One of my canoeing partners discovered a great spot this way. I remember it vividly because the experience was so unusual.

We were on a large lake, paddling from one campsite to the next. My companion was determined to keep a lure in the water. We went hours without experiencing any action at all.

Suddenly a six-pound northern struck his lure, a floating plug. A few days afterwards, on our return route, we caught more in the same place. A year later, I revisited this location on another trip with another partner. Results were also good.

We had wandered into a great spot, thirty feet off a fealureless shoreline. We would have needed ESP to know it was there. I wish I had had a mask and snorkel to study what features lay below.

That experience, notwithstanding, I think trolling slows down canoe travel to a degree that far outweighs its fishing effectiveness. Dragging a lure behind the boat as you travel from one campsite to the next is a surprisingly low-percentage operation.

If you troll with a plan, you should expect to pick up a fish every quarter mile or so. If you troll randomly while you travel from one campsite to the next, you may go all day without a single fish.

Lastly, when you get a strike while trolling, if circumstances permit, screen thc area more thoroughly by casting. This frequently produces additional fish.

CHAPTER 7

SIX CLASSIC CASTING SPOTS

I've never seen a good spot that didn't conform to the principle of two or more features coming together. The following sorts of areas, however, are particularly worth investigating.

1. Weed Beds

Large weed beds in reasonably deep water are great. Look for at least four feet on one side. Fish hide in the dense, aquatic vegetation. They seem to look out into more open water, particularly on the deeper side, anticipating that forage will expose itself. Casting parallel to the edge of the bed may expose the silhouette of your lure to a fish waiting in ambush.

With special lures, you can cast right into the weeds themselves. I've had very good luck casting a weed-less spoon tipped with a plastic worm into thick weeds. You do need a stout rod with a fast action, meaning it only bends for about the top quarter, to set the hook under these conditions.

2. Cliffs

The face of a cliff as it enters a lake is often overlooked. Wind brings forage up to the cliff, where it can go no farther. Often there will be resting places below the waves where a fish may wait for a meal to float into its neighborhood.

By positioning the canoe a few feet off from the cliffs, casting parallel, and moving forward every few casts, this particular feature can be tested quickly. Not all cliffs have good resting places, but the right ones can be extremely productive.

3. Current Lines

If you are fishing where there are rapids or riffles, often the best bet is to beach the canoe and cast from shore. Such areas on rivers can be excellent and it is well worth taking a break from paddling in order to give them a try.

Forage, such as minnows, crayfish, worms, and insects all may be adrift in moving water. Fish wait in small resting places near the current, which is the functional equivalent of a moving buffet.

Good fish can be found in surprisingly small places. I remember a pool at the end of a portage. It was about four feet deep. A shallow rapid flowed in and created an eddy, which was perhaps twenty feet long. The river itself was navigable but was barely more than a creek.

After we finished carrying our gear across, we took a break. My canoe partner went to the head of the pool, stood on a rock, cast downstream, and retrieved a jig and spinner upstream, close to the eddy line. We knew a thin layer of still water probably lay along the bottom.

My friend didn't expect much. Really, he was just fooling around, even though this was an obvious spot and a convenient one. Suddenly, a big northern pike smashed his lure. We hooted with excitement when we saw the size of it. We didn't have a scale, but I would estimate it to have been a good five pounds.

At the time, we were astonished to find such a large fish resting on the bottom of a relatively small eddy. Today, I appreciate that it may have been the best habitat in quite a distance. A large predator had moved in from a lake and staked out a claim.

4. Eddies and Foamed Eddies

Eddies are classic areas on rivers. An eddy that has accumulated foam is a particularly high percentage spot. Fish like to rest right underneath.

Casting downstream, while working the current line near deeper water is productive. Sometimes working the edge of the eddy close to shore is productive too.

Although it can be more difficult to control, casting upstream is a little better. Fish tend to look into the current, while waiting for food to appear in their strike zone.

When casting to a current line and eddy, use the first cast to test the upper part of the water column. Then, work the lure near the bottom.

A spinnerbait is an excellent search lure to test both levels of water. If the depth is five feet or less, however, a jointed plug is usually more effective.

5. Tops of Pools

Casting perpendicular to shore can be a deadly technique near the top of a pool, especially if there is a bit of an eddy where it begins. Again, placing your lure within a foot of shore generally yields the highest percentage of fish.

6. Exits of Pools

A bit of deeper water a few feet in front of the rapid at the outlet of a pool also can be extremely productive. Cast a few inches into the rapid and begin a retrieve upstream into the pool. Magic can happen.

7. The Calm Layer on the Bottom

Moving water by itself is a unique structure. It is counter intuitive, but rapids often have two layers. The fast moving water on top may not go all the way to the bottom. Often there is a layer of calm water right on the bottom. Scientists, if they know a few measurements, can use a formula to calculate how deep it will be.

Steep-pass fish ladders are designed to take advantage of this phenomenon. The top layer of water looks crazy. Fish can easily zip right up, however, using the calmer water below.

Unlike current, a calm layer of water on the bottom can't be directly observed. This, however, is where fish hang out. They may come off the bottom to feed on forage caught in the turbulence. Or, more likely, they will wait for food to reach them before they partake.

Although it may require a moment or two of thought to develop a strategy for presenting a lure or bait, this calm layer is one of the most potentially productive spots to consider when evaluating fish-holding areas on a river, both for casting and trolling.

CHAPTER 8

THREE CLASSIC TROLLING AREAS

Three classic areas on lakes and rivers lend themselves to trolling. They all have one easily observed feature and a reasonably good chance of other features intersecting at some unobservable point.

1. Rapids (Within Reason)

Extensive areas of calm water exist under moving water. A large feature such as this consistently holds fish, but they won't be everywhere.

A rapid may extend for a half mile or so, but fish will only be found in a few ideal holding places. For this reason, trolling, within reason, is the best search technique. I say, "Within reason" because there is an obvious safety issue. Don't even think about trolling a rapid if both paddlers are needed to control the boat.

It is not uncommon, however, to find water that is moving swiftly, yet is reasonably straight and not too rough. Such conditions lend themselves well to trolling and exploring the calmer layer below.

This is not a situation for dangling. Even under the best circumstances, rear paddlers should have their fishing equipment completely secured, meaning no hooks exposed. Front paddlers should have their rods in a rod holder in the front of the boat and at least one hand on their paddles.

A crankbait is an ideal trolling lure for river rapids. The fat body of a crank wobbles and yet is stable in current. The lip of a crank pulls it down. I think a crank designed to run at two to four feet below the surface is best for most situations. You want to feel it hit the bottom every so often.

The lip will bounce off objects on the bottom and so is resistant to snagging. Resistant, however, is the operative word. Inevitably, that lure will hang. The rear paddler then must maneuver the boat upstream while the front paddler manages the pole until the lure can be released. This can become challenging. For safety reasons, it is especially important that only one outfit be rigged.

This trolling technique appears counterintuitive, unless you know about the calm layer of water below. When you hit a spot that holds fish, it can be extremely productive.

I once caught six smallmouths within about a quarter mile. I'd have a fish on within half a minute of release and resetting the crank in the current. If I'd had a mask and snorkel, I would have gone back to see what made this rapid so exceptional.

2. Rocky Shorelines

Almost any rocky shoreline with a drop-off is worth trolling. Somewhere, somehow another feature will intersect and likely hold fish. As you cruise along such a place, you will often encounter water deeper than ten feet. Accordingly, it's hard to beat a bottom-bouncing sinker and a shallow running plug as a search lure. The plug should be attached about three feet back from the sinker.

You want to keep your lure in the general neighborhood of the depth change as much as possible. Sometimes it's better to be on shallow side. Sometimes, it's better to be on the deep side. Meandering gives your lure the best chance of being at the right place at the right time.

People are naturally inclined to troll too far from shore. I think starting about five feet away, and then trying to identify the drop-off works best. It is unusual to want to be farther than twenty feet from shore.

3. Peninsulas

A peninsula extending into a lake provides another classic trolling situation. There's a good chance it extends underwater, creating a three sided drop-off that may go out for a long distance. There's no way to know where the depth change may intersect other features and attract fish.

A bottom-bouncing sinker and plug is again an ideal search lure, considering the unpredictable depth changes. Start on one side of the peninsula near the shore. Go out a hundred yards in a loop, cross back, and end on the opposite side of the peninsula.

CHAPTER 9

THE FISH OF THE GREAT NORTH

On a wilderness canoe trip, you are often traveling through extraordinary habitat. The possibilities are exciting. The most common species are smallmouth bass, walleyes, and northern pike. These are the magnificent fish of the north woods.

As you proceed farther towards the Arctic, you will begin to encounter large brook trout, lake trout, arctic char, and even salmon. They, too, are magnificent fish, which somehow personify the cold, primeval, even magical nature of those ecosystems.

All these fish follow the same approximate rules in locating themselves. All may be caught using the same types of lures and tackle. In my opinion, there is just no need to think about specialized presentations.

It is common to catch fish weighing more than two pounds out in the bush. So, as a normal practice, larger lures are the order of the day.

Panfish, such as yellow perch, rock bass, bluegills, and crappie, are of secondary interest. They are fun to catch, however, and good to eat. I always take along a few smaller lures and floats, otherwise known as bobbers. Additionally, a few small lures may become useful if you find yourself in trout water.

My personal favorite fish is the yellow perch's larger cousin, the walleye. They taste great, fight well, and commonly grow to a good size. What is not to like?

Northern pike are also excellent. Being aggressive predators, they tend to become common in any water system they inhabit. They are by far the easiest to catch. They grow to a good size, so, as with walleyes, you don't need many to feed a group of people.

One may be enough. I had the good fortune to catch a nine-pound pike on one of my trips. It provided a generous serving of fillets to four hungry canoeists.

Pike do have more bones, but it is not difficult to fillet them, so the extra bones are really not an issue. Pike are just a little bland, but they are still an excellent eating fish on the trail.

Smallmouth bass are not shy about biting. They jump, and fight harder per pound than any other fish. They are a joy to catch. For unknown reasons, smallmouths are rarely eaten, but I can attest that properly filleted, breaded, and fried, they are excellent.

Photo by Rodney Goodwill

Brook trout, lake trout, and arctic char are all cousins. They and the ecosystems they inhabit are fascinating. Although they are a joy to catch, rumors about their being good to eat are greatly overstated. Yes, it can be done, but in my opinion, trout are at best an appetizer.

Salmon, on the other hand, are arguably the best tasting fish there are. If you have the amazing good fortune to catch a salmon out in the bush, you are in for the camping equivalent of gourmet dining, especially if you still have some red wine left in your Duluth pack.

CHAPTER 10

RODS AND REELS

What type of outfit do you take on a canoe trip? How do you pack it securely and keep it accessible while you are on the water?

If you expect a lot of portaging, you need to find a minimalist approach. Otherwise, although you still want to be well-organized, you can take along more gear.

Bait casting and closed-faced spinning reels work well, but I think open-faced spinning gear is more versatile. It lends itself to two-handed casting, which is helpful in many situations.

On most routes you have the possibility of connecting with fish weighing five to even ten pounds. As enjoyable as light tackle may be, it isn't really appropriate for good-sized northern pikes or walleyes.

Accordingly, I recommend heavy tackle, including high quality monofilament line rated at twenty to thirty pounds. I also recommend putting a pair of needle-nosed pliers in your waist pack. They can be invaluable for removing hooks from a nasty, big-toothed fish.

I recommend poles designed for lures with a minimum of a fourth of an ounce and a maximum of about five-eighths of an ounce. The range is usually written on the side of the rod. You can use lures that are a little lighter or a little heavier.

Additionally you need to consider how much bend is in the rod. The more bend, generally, the farther you can cast. The less bend, the easier you can set the hook. This is important if you are fishing with jigs or plastic worms. Myself, I prefer rods that bend about halfway down.

There are many, many good rods on the market. I will say "Ugly Stiks" are nearly unbreakable, have good performance characteristics, and are relatively inexpensive. It is, however, hard to go wrong when buying a rod.

I do think high-end graphite rods tend to be a little too fragile on the trail. I have also tried collapsible fishing rods, breaking three before giving up on the idea.

An often overlooked detail is checking line before you leave home. It should be between one-sixteenth and one-eighth inch from the edge of the spool. Additionally, at home, you should use a swivel to attach the line to a fixed point and back up with the rod in hand until the spool is empty. Then, reel in with the line under tension. Doing this will save aggravation on the trail, although occasional bird's nests are all but inevitable.

Lastly, you want to test the reel's drag setting. A light pull on the swivel should be enough to slowly release line. Typically, it takes a couple of hours at home to properly set up your rod, select lures, and organize your tackle.

In my opinion, it is just too inconvenient to stow and break out fly fishing gear in a canoe. You miss too many spontaneous opportunities to cast. Fly fishing is, however, an elegant, almost addictive, way to fish. In general, people interested in fly fishing already have advanced skills. They know what they are getting into.

Whatever you bring, I recommend stowing it in a rod and reel case. Packed in a canoe with bags of camping equipment, your gear will take an unbelievable pounding. The case keeps everything organized and at least semi-protected.

The case is also a safety precaution. You can keep the lure inside, bonneted, and zipped. You don't have to worry about hooks getting snagged on packs. Even more importantly, you don't need to worry about becoming impaled by a treble hook, if you capsize.

A case can be quickly attached to a thwart, if you see potentially problematic water ahead. Cases, however, usually float, so you are always at less risk of losing your gear, if you dump unexpectedly.

Enter "rod and reel case" into an Internet search engine and you will see many choices. A case that includes an extra pocket to stow a small waist pack for lures and accessories may prove exceptionally useful.

If access and egress require travel by commercial airline, a case may be just a littlc too much. Then, a rod and reel can be packed in other luggage and later secured under a thwart with a small bungee cord. It's a workable, albeit a less desirable system.

CHAPTER 11

LURES

When thinking about what lure to use, ask yourself how well a particular lure matches the task at hand. Usually, you want to be able to cover a lot of water without snagging, and keep the lure in a zone where there may be fish.

Crankbaits are great. They dive on a retrieve or in current because of water pressure on their lip. They wobble, yet are stable. On the trail, I remove the front treble hook on a crank. (The extra treble occasionally entangles the line.) That makes casting easier and seems to have no effect on hookups.

I use hook bonnets to help keep cranks and other lures with treble hooks organized safely. Bonnets are available in most catalogues, such as Cabela's or Bass Pro Shops. They are plastic shields into which a treble hook may be inserted.

Spinnerbaits are versatile speed lures that allow you to cover a large area. In addition, such speed tends to provoke aggressive assaults.

High-quality spinnerbaits are made with higher quality components, particularly the swivels on the spinning blades. They cost more, but the higher functionality of the blade makes them well worth the extra expense.

The hook runs with the point on top, which lends itself to both snag resistance and a high percentage of hookups. Rarely does a fish weighing more than a pound strike and not get hooked.

Spinnerbaits don't snag often. If the vegetation is really thick, however, a weedless spoon tipped with plastic is better suited to the conditions. If the area is relatively weedless, then a big, flashy French spinner can be more functional. Those big blades can attract fish from quite a distance.

If I could only take one lure on a trip, I would take a quarter-ounce jig. While not perfect in every situation, it can be used effectively in most.

Similarly, you will almost never go wrong with a small spoon or blade bait. Any species of fish will take them. They cast like bullets, and are easy to control as you retrieve. They, too, can be made to work under almost any conditions.

If I expect panfish or trout along a route, I pack a couple of small French spinners, which are exceptionally effective on trout.

I have often encountered situations where the specialized nature of floating plugs makes them clearly the tool of choice. I remember casting a crankbait downstream into the head of a rapid once. Actually, I couldn't cast quite far enough so I had to let it float the last twenty feet or so.

I retrieved, with the idea that the lip on the crank would take my lure about four feet down and I would be able to test the calm layer on the bottom, right in front of the rapid.

My logic was good. Almost immediately, I hooked a large fish. I thought it would be a northern pike or perhaps a walleye. I was astonished to pull in a four to five pound brook trout. I didn't have a scale with me. I have, however, caught several brook trout that weighed two pounds and this one was much, much bigger. It resembled an oversized football with fins.

I was on the famous Rupert River in Quebec. Later, I did some research and discovered that this area was famous for large brook trout.

I got to fish again the next evening. I used a gold, quarter-ounce blade bait, thinking it would be better for trout. I went to a small rapid. I cast downstream and retrieved slowly up a current line.

As my reward for getting smart and trying a more logical trout lure, I hooked onto a nine pound northern. I landed that fish, but not before it straightened one set of the small hooks on that tiny lure.

The blade bait would have been a great choice for a trout, and it served its purpose with a large pike. It got into the zone and provoked a strike. I would, however, have been better off sticking with a large crankbait or jointed minnow.

Although people invariably develop preferences, it is misguided to think that one type of lure is generically superior to another. A lure is a tool to find fish, and it should be selected according to the circumstances at hand.

I do think most people take too many lures with them out into the bush. Surprisingly, it is unusual to lose one. Personally, I usually take a crankbait, a jointed minnow, a high-quality spinnerbait, a large French spinner, a blade bait, a quarter-ounce spoon, a weedless spoon, and three jigs in different sizes (one-fourth, one-eighth, one-sixteenth).

For trolling, I also take along a half-ounce bottom-bouncing sinker pre-rigged with a minnow-shaped plug with a small lip.

CHAPTER 12

ACCESSORIES

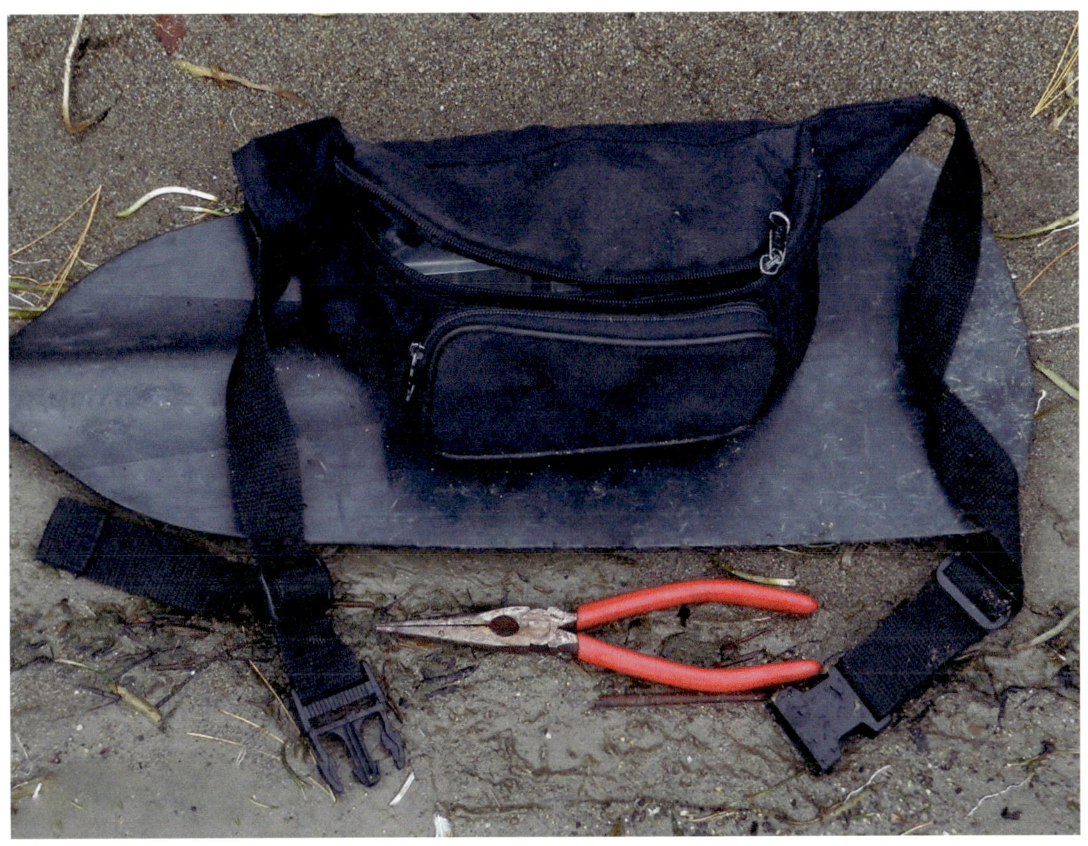

The Waist Pack

On my early trips, I packed my stuff in a tackle box, just like I did when fishing near home. On the trail, however, this wasn't anywhere nearly as functional.

The tackle box had a tendency to come open and spill lures on the floor of the canoe. It was awkward to carry around on shore or portage. I often needed something only to discover that my gear was a distance away.

Eventually I capsized, which revealed another problem. It sank with everything in it, and maybe fifty dollars worth of lures. I was not happy.

God was, however, merciful. We dumped near the shore in crystal clear water. The latch stayed securely closed. I watched in amazement as my paddling partner floated above, flexed his legs perpendicular to the surface, dove maybe six feet, and retrieved everything.

That happy outcome notwithstanding, the experience convinced me that I needed to try something else. I eventually bought a small waist pack and a few compartmentalized plastic boxes. That solution has stood the test of decades.

I use one plastic box for bigger lures and snap swivels. I take a second plastic box for smaller lures that I may not use as often.

Wearing it in front while you are fishing keeps everything conveniently at hand. It can be quickly secured to a thwart or stuffed into a larger bag.

A small chest pack is a similar solution to the problem of keeping gear handy and well organized. I prefer a small waist pack, but, depending on your preference, a chest pack designed for fishing is well worth considering.

Nail Clippers

Nail clippers are an easily overlooked, but extremely handy accessory. A primary nail clipper should be kept in your pocket. The one in your tackle is a back-up. I also bring a pair of needle-nosed pliers.

Snap Swivels

Jigs and spinnerbaits should be tied directly to the line. Other lures should be attached with a snap swivel to reduce problems associated with twisting line. Use a clinch knot for both swivels and lures. Directions are conveniently available on a variety of websites.

Snap swivels are an important accessory. I learned this the hard way by tying a French spinner directly to my line once. The experiment failed miserably.

After just a few casts, my reel became a "bird's nest" of tangled monofilament. Completely beyond rehabilitation, I eventually had to throw the line away and re-spool. Similarly, I once tried trolling a jointed plug with no swivel and got the same result.

I recommend using swivels large enough so that you can easily attach and detach lures. Within reason, I don't think you gain anything by using very small swivels, even on smaller lures.

On one trip, I watched my canoe partner take a beaten-up, small spoon out of his tackle box. It looked like something he bought at a yard sale for less than a dollar. He attached it to a really large swivel, one you might use on the ocean. It was a third as big as his lure. In combination, they were a ghastly looking affair.

Honesty compels me to acknowledge that he caught more fish than I did, in part because he was fishing almost constantly. His success made me appreciate how irrelevant finesse fishing techniques often are to the conditions you may encounter on a remote canoe trip.

I recommend packing accessories such as a rod holder, a pre-rigged bottom-bouncing sinker, and extra line separately. You want them to be conveniently available. You don't, however, use them often enough to keep them on your person in a waist pack.

Rod Holders

Because you need to paddle, you can't always personally control your fishing equipment with your hands. If you have no choice, you can place the rod under your knee or wedge it between your gear and a thwart.

A rod holder makes many things much easier. In particular, it makes it easier to "dangle" a lure over the side of a canoe while the rear person paddles. Similarly, a rod holder makes it possible to troll in current more conveniently and safely.

Unfortunately, most models weigh about a pound and they take up space. You have to decide whether you will use it enough to make it worth the extra trouble. If a route contains frequent portaging, rod holders are almost always more bother than they are worth.

There is usually no practical alternative to a clamp-on rod holder. Although an enterprising person could find a way to secure a mounting plate to a gunnel or thwart, that would only work for a personal canoe. It is common, however, to find yourself in someone else's canoe, especially on a remote trip.

Unfortunately, most clamp-on rod holders are designed for boats and often don't adapt well to canoes. I have had good luck with a "Down-Easter" on heavy Royalex boats. It has an especially sturdy clamp.

The rails and thwarts for different canoes vary. Generally, heavier Royalex canoes have bigger rails and thwarts than those made of lightweight Kevlar. A clamp well suited to a Royalex boat may not attach properly to a lighter Kevlar one.

Bringing a block of wood, about one inch thick, three inches wide, and four inches long to use as a shim can be helpful. There is, however, a product sized for the smaller rails and thwarts of a lightweight canoe. Known as the "Rod Sentry," it is uniquely designed and well worth considering.

Entering "Down-Easter Rod Holder" or "Rod Sentry" into an Internet search engine should locate many vendors. There are, however, other worthy products on the market.

I will say that many clamps are not rugged enough to handle a ten-pound fish without dislodging from the canoe. I recommend consulting the catalogue of a well-established company and being prepared to experiment. It may take some time to locate the rod holder that best suits your needs.

I almost always take a rod holder, if I am reasonably confident that there will be time and good places enough to use one. Otherwise, I defer to the need for limiting the amount of gear I pack for a trip.

Trolling Sinkers

Lastly, bottom-bouncing sinkers are another accessory worth mentioning. They facilitate trolling in deeper water. I have had very good results with a Gapen "Bait-Walker" and a Lindy "No-Snagg."

In a motorized boat, heavier sinkers would be in order, but it is unusual to encounter a need for a big sinker in a canoe. A half-ounce weight works well almost all the time.

CHAPTER 13

MISCELLANEOUS TECHNIQUES

Basic techniques, such as casting perpendicular to the shore, casting to the top and bottoms of rapids, and running lures up and down current lines all work well.

There are, however, other methods to try, involving less active presentations of a lure. These techniques may entice less aggressive fish into striking.

Dangling

Dangling is a common example of a more passive method to put a lure in the strike zone and entice. Almost all lures can be dangled. For this purpose, however, I prefer spinnerbaits, jigs with spinners, and blade baits.

Slow, Stop, and Go

Another good passive technique is a "slow, stop, and go" retrieve. Try casting a jointed plug near the shoreline. Let it rest for a minute. Twitch. Then retrieve a couple of feet. Rest the lure for thirty seconds. Then, twitch and repeat. The retrieve should be parallel, but angled slightly offshore. It should take a few minutes per cast to complete. This technique works especially well if the water is calm.

Float Fishing

They used to be called bobbers. Now, the terms "float" or even "strike indicator" are used more commonly. Float fishing is well worth studying. It only looks simple.

Fishing catalogues carry modern floats and devices to attach them to your line. On flat water, I recommend setting the bait about a foot below the float.

A small jig tipped with live bait, plastic, or even a maggot-sized slice of cheese works great. A slow retrieve is in order once again. It is a great way to fish. Though it is counterintuitive, large fish will take a tiny jig tipped with something and suspended beneath a float.

For a river, I recommend setting the depth at about two-thirds the length of your pole. You want your lure or bait to drift along the calm layer on the bottom. I think rigging the float fixed on moving water works better. Spacing a few split shot sinkers on the line is sometimes needed to get the jig to the bottom.

If you are exploring the edge of a current or eddy, it is great to let the float slip downstream, stop, wait a moment, then let it slip downstream another five feet and pause again. You can work as much as thirty or so feet of water this way.

It is best to keep the line between the float and the rod out of the water. That way the float is affected primarily by the jig below, rather than by the pull of the water on your line.

At camp, you sometimes can use the rod holder to hold your rod and reel on the canoe. Cast out and wait, watch the sunset, and drink a cup of wine. The float provides a little extra entertainment.

Cookies

For a quick way of ascertaining whether fish are in the area, try taking a cookie, crumpling it into crumbs, and throwing it to a spot on the water. Small pieces of bread may also be used for this purpose.

The result can be illuminating. Often, unexpectedly, the water will simply boil with little fish. That's a good sign. More likely than not, it means bigger fish will be in the same general area.

CHAPTER 14

EATING FISH

With all due respect to humans being the apex predator, the moment of capture is the moment of emotional completion. Returning prey is every bit as satisfying as killing it to eat.

Virtually all serious anglers practice catch and release—as though it were a religion. On a longer trip, however, where taking steaks in coolers just isn't practical, I think a strong case can be made for eating fish as often as possible.

Dry food has come a long ways since I began canoeing. Between the grocery store and specialty supply houses, a modern camper is eating a luxurious diet by historical standards. Dry food packagers, however, have never been able to do a great job with protein.

After a few days on the water, your body will crave a return to real food. You will feel much better if you get fresh, unprocessed protein into your system. I consider fish to be a substantial addition to a canoeist's nutrition, especially on a longer trip.

Pack a few brown paper lunch bags and some seasoned bread crumbs. Put the fish pieces in the lunch bag and shake to coat with crumbs. Fry in hot oil.

This simple method is absolutely delicious. Fried potatoes, a packet of brown rice with vegetables, even a packet of spaghetti with tomato sauce, all go together great with fish.

To fillet, you need a special fillet knife. It is important to use the tip of the blade to separate flesh from rib bones. I recommend leaving the tail attached until the last step, which is taking off the skin. A regular hunting knife may work better on some of the big cuts, especially on a larger fish.

Almost anyone can quickly learn to fillet. Many videos and books are available, and directions often come with a fillet knife. It is easiest, however, to enter "filleting fish" into an Internet search engine. Many good video clips will appear.

CHAPTER 15

CLOSING

When I was a kid, I would grab a rod from the garage, put some worms in a can, and walk up the driveway. My friends and I could go for miles into the woods, almost from our doorsteps.

Today, we travel long distances and have acquired garages full of tackle. We personify that old joke about the difference between a child and an adult being that the adult has more expensive toys.

Although I still really enjoy fishing in familiar places near my home, traveling, interacting with new people, and experimenting with new techniques have all become fascinating adjuncts to the experience.

Today, fishing is a large-scale industry. The technology that put a man on the moon has been applied to fishing gear. The equipment available to an ordinary person would have been beyond the imagination of even the wealthiest individuals a hundred years ago.

With today's Internet, DVDs, magazines, and constant innovations in tackle, we are assured of always having something different and exciting to try. Fishing is a gift that keeps on giving, a stimulating learning process that never ends.

My experiences have confirmed the general wisdom of that Chippewa guide's understated observation, "It takes a while." It is a pleasure, however, to remain a student.

One of the best places to learn is ***In-Fisherman***. In addition to the magazine, there is a TV show, and a constantly expanding catalogue of books and DVDs. Although, many good magazines, books, and videos are published by other businesses, there may be no other place where so much high quality information is centralized. There has never been anything quite like it.

Finally, I will assert that there is a joy in taking care of the fishery. In the wild, the apex predator plays a central role in maintaining the health of its prey species. In a high-tech parallel, today's sports, through clubs and organizations, play a central role in preserving fish and wildlife, way more than an uninitiated observer would be likely to suspect.

A large percentage of outdoor people belong to organizations that promote good practices and conservation. In my opinion, **the Nature Conservancy** is one of the best because it is exclusively devoted to preserving wild places, that is, habitat. A membership is well worth the fee.

Other groups, such as **Trout Unlimited** and **Ducks Unlimited**, do a great job of combining a national umbrella organization with strong regional chapters engaged in specific projects. They offer an opportunity, as the expression goes, to "think globally and act locally."

Sporting clubs can be a tangible, personally rewarding way to become involved. For example, in my hometown the Andover Fish and Game Club is exceptionally productive.

Regional land trusts, such as the Kennebec Land Trust in Maine, where I live today, are another tangible personally rewarding way to get involved.

Should you start to get interested, I recommend joining an organization of your choice. First, simply sign up and pay dues. Later, after you've had a chance to scope things out, you may want to begin going to meetings, joining the board of directors, or even becoming an officer. Doing these things isn't a duty or an obligation. Instead, think of these opportunities as intensely pleasurable aspects of fishing, canoeing, hunting, and other outdoor pursuits.

Made in the USA
Columbia, SC
09 May 2025